THE JOURNAL OF A CLIMBER

Understanding Life's Journey

Chuck Reaves, CSP, CPAE

**Executive
Books**

Journal of a Climber

Published by
Executive Books
206 West Allen Street
Mechanicsburg, PA 17055
717-766-9499   800-233-2665
Fax: 717-766-6565
www.ExecutiveBooks.com

ISBN: 978-1-933715-66-7

Printed in the United States of America

Table of Contents

1

Today I begin my climb of Mount Majority.

*All of my life I have been told that every person must make
their mark by joining those who have gone before. Mount
Majority looms out in the distance and dominates the hori-
zon. It is as far as anyone can see. There is nothing beyond
Mount Majority; at least that is what I have always heard.*

*The climb will not be easy, I know, but I am prepared. I
have my schooling behind me and I have packed all of the
provisions I will need for the climb.*

*In my knapsack there is water, food, matches, some clothes
and such. I have the basic tools I will need. I have a small
tent strapped to the knapsack – the kind of tent that everyone carries on such a trip.*

*Today I will leave Base Camp where I have spent my entire
life. I grew up here. My school and its teachers are here.
My church and my religious leaders are here. This is the
only life I have known so far. Still, I have always known
that at one point in all of our lives, everyone must go out
and make a life for himself or herself and that life is on
Mount Majority. That is where most people live the best
days of their lives.*

*Mount Majority is where the majority of people live. Some
people stay in Base Camp to prepare others for the climb,
but the others move on to Mount Majority.*

*I have heard the stories about people who tried to venture
past Mount Majority. Some tried and were never heard*

*form again, others went mad. There really is nothing be-
yond Mount Majority, you know.*

*I am prepared, I am packed and now it is time to begin the
climb. Part of me is excited about the certain adventure
that awaits me. The fact that I will now be my own person –
a grown-up – and will have the respect of my peers and
elders is also important.*

*Along with the excitement comes the fear. There is the fear
of the unknown, the uncertainty of whether or not I can really make it. Just because others have successfully made
the climb does not mean that I will. What if I fail?*

*There are many ways to fail, I've been taught. In fact, there
are more ways to fail than there are to succeed so it is wise
to take the safe and proven approach to climbing the
Mount. Taking risks in the climb can cause a person bodily
injury or even death. If the worst does not happen, a risk-
taker could still be saddled with a lifetime of embarrass-
ment and ridicule for having tried something foolish.*

*There are stones along the path and one misstep can result
in a crippling injury. Some people who tried to climb the
Mount suffered these crippling injuries. As a result, they
hobbled back down the mountain and had to resign themselves to a life here in Base Camp, unable to make the
climb. They will spend their lives in the most menial of
jobs, all because one mistake ended their chances to live
with the others on Mount Majority.*

*Oh, some of them say someone else tripped them or they
were the victims of inadequate preparation, or something.
The truth is that we all begin here at Base Camp and <u>we</u>
determine whether or not we will be successful on our*

climb. Still, I do not want to be one of the ones who ends up back here spending their life in some miserable, menial job.

I will begin my climb up Mount Majority, but I will not take any chances. That is the surest way to success.

After a lifetime, of preparation, today I begin my climb of Mount Majority.

2

The climb so far has been uneventful but I have learned a lot.

Every day I pass some people and every day some people pass me. I seem to be climbing faster than some and slower than others. There is no rhyme or reason to the faster and the slower people. Some who pass me are older than I and some of the people I pass are younger than I.

Some people seem to be traveling slowly on purpose. They stop frequently to admire the view or to examine the flowers and shrubs along the trail. They see no reason not to stop and help others who are having difficulties even if it costs them precious time. For them, I guess, the journey is more important than the destination.

Some of the people who seem to be the most physically fit for this climb are taking longer to make the climb than others. Some stop along the way to rest and to play. Others just seem to be loping along at an easy pace, not really motivated to reach the top of Mount Majority. That seems strange to me. Why doesn't everyone want to reach the pinnacle as soon as possible?

Some people complain the entire trip. They complain about the weather. If it is raining, they complain about being wet. If it is sunny, they complain about being hot. They complain about the difficulty of the climb and the fact that others seem to have it so much easier. They stop to commiserate with others who seem to be as unhappy as they are. Why can't they see that we are all pretty much alike and the trip is really no easier for one person than another?

Complaining only makes the climb seem longer. Stopping to spend time in conversations with other unhappy people only reinforces the attitude that the climb is hard. And it wastes precious time.

Some people struggle because they were not prepared for the climb. Some lack knowledge and some lack provisions. The ones who lack knowledge have only themselves to blame, the way I see it. Back in Base Camp, knowledge was always available for those who wanted to learn. Some people chose to disregard those learning opportunities and now they find themselves on the climb lacking some essential knowledge.

Those who lack provisions may not have had the resources back in Base Camp that the others did and could not afford the necessities. Those of us along the trail who have encountered these people have shared our provisions, as much as we can. I find myself more willing to help those who offer to help carry my knapsack in return for supplies than those who seem to think that the rest of us owe them something. I don't ever let someone else carry my supplies, of course, but still I prefer to help those who make the offer.

I have noticed a few people who are zig-zagging their way up the slopes. They cut across in front of me and behind me. I can hear them muttering to themselves that the path must be easier on one side or the other. It is strange that one person will cross from my right to my left thinking they are going to find an easier way and, almost immediately, someone crosses in the opposite direction for exactly the same reason. Can't they see that choosing a course and staying on it is faster, shorter and ultimately easier than zig-zagging back and forth? They frequently run from one good thing to another, or so they think.

The most remarkable people are the Sherpas. These indigenous people travel almost effortlessly up and down the slope. I only see them from time to time and sometimes go weeks without ever seeing one. Other climbers have told me that they have never seen one while some say they see Sherpas frequently. The Sherpas will do whatever you ask them to do, must they must be paid in their own currency. Most of us do not carry their currency so we cannot take advantage of their help. They are strange people, these Sherpas. They rarely speak and when they look at you their expressions are neither smiles nor frowns. It is as if they are looking right through you.

There are times when the climb is more difficult. Clouds come in frequently and obscure the way. By the time the clouds have lifted, many of us find ourselves off course and have to veer back.

Then there are times when the slope becomes very steep. When that happens we have to make a choice. We can either put in the extra effort to climb the steeper slopes or we can try to circle around the side of the mountain and try to find an easier path.

I tried the easier path once. It took longer and the path was still almost as steep. I decided then to just tackle every challenge as it appeared.

So now a routine is setting in. I arise at about the same time each day. I do the same things each day in preparation for the day's climb. I climb for the same amount of time and then settle in for another evening.

About every seventh day I come across a stream where I can fill my water bottles. Enough fruit and berries and such grow along the trail to easily sustain us climbers. Some-times we have to walk away from the trail or scale up a tree to find it, but it's always around somewhere. (The com-plainers complain about that also.)

It is late, I am tired, and tomorrow is another day of climbing.

3

Today was a tough day.

The weather was bad – as bad as I have seen. My feet are sore and my hands are chapped. I feel as though I have aged a lot since leaving Base Camp and Mount Majority seems to be an even larger hurdle than when I left. While I know I am getting closer, it still seems far away.

I can look back and see Base camp. Sometimes in the evenings when I am tired from a long day's climb, I look back and wonder if staying in Base Camp is really such a bad thing. It is true that the people there do not reach Majority, but they don't have to struggle every day either.

What made today worse was seeing another climber, about the same age as I am, on the side of the path. He had stumbled and fallen. He was bruised all over. His face showed the signs of a long hard climb and the frustration of finding himself down on the ground. I noticed the swollen ankle. It happens when someone carelessly steps on a rock and their foot turns inside or outside. For many people it is the type of injury that can send them back down to Base Camp. And for most who return to Base Camp, there is never another day of climbing.

I stood some distance from the downed climber. I did not want to get too close but I don't know why. Maybe being too close would make me a part of their situation or something. Anyway I took my break, drank some water and just stood and stared at the climber's predicament, happy to be standing.

Another pair of climbers joined me and we talked quietly about the poor climber and what his ultimate fate might be.

"There but for the grace of God go I," one of them said as he made his way on up the slope.

Tonight as I prepared my meal, I thought about the injured climber and the remark made by the other climber. Is that what this is really all about? Is it simply God's grace or the luck of the draw that determines who wins and who loses?

That does not seem fair, somehow.

Why bother preparing ourselves in Base Camp or struggling to make the climb at all if the only determining factor for success is something we cannot control?

Maybe I am just tired from the climb. Maybe I am frustrated.

Mount Majority is much higher than it appears form Base Camp. This journey is taking much longer than I had imagined. Still, I am making progress – better than some, not as much as others. But I am progressing. At least I am not lying injured by the side of the path.

Tonight I can barely see the lights at Base Camp. It is a reminder that I am making progress.

A young climber is camping beside me tonight. He left Base Camp long after I did. He is very fit and able and will reach Mount Majority before I do.

I have shared some of the things I have learned on my climb and he told me some of the news from Base Camp.

They are still teaching the same things there and it seems little has changed. Maybe when some of the injured climbers return to Base Camp they can help the people there teach more useful lessons, ones that will help future climbers.

But I don't recall the people there using lessons from injured climbers when I was in Base Camp. After all, who wants to sit at the feet and learn from someone who failed?

4

<u>A most remarkable day!</u>

I had hardly begun my climb this morning when it happened. The sun was up, the air was cool and there was a slight breeze. It was the perfect day for climbing and I had big plans for covering a lot of ground. I was humming to myself and totally enjoying the beauty of the day and the joy of climbing.

Apparently I was not being careful because I stepped on a rock and fell face first onto a slab of granite. I think I may have been unconscious for a moment. When I gathered my senses, I could hardly move my arm, my hands were scratched and bruised. I felt blood running down my face.

And then I became aware of the pain in my foot. I looked and saw that my ankle was swollen up to several times its normal size. It was black and blue and it hurt.

I let out a scream, put my hands on my head and fell back on the ground.

Then it hit me. This was the end of the climb for me.

I lay there for hours. I used my water and a cloth to clean my face and hands. But they were the least of my worries. My ankle only began to hurt more and to look worse.

In the early afternoon I heard a noise and looked off to the other side of the trail. A climber had stopped to take a break and was staring at me. In a moment other climbers joined the first. They spoke in hushed tones and then resumed their climb up Mount Majority.

By the late afternoon the sun was beating down on my head. I lay there with my eyes closed, wondering what life would be like after this. I became aware of a shadow coming over me. I opened my eyes and was surprised to see a Sherpa standing over me. As they always do, he just looked at me, expressionless.

We just stared at each other for what seemed to be an hour, but I know it was only a few moments. We seemed to be communicating, without words, but communicating. He seemed to be hearing more than I, if that is possible.

His eyes never left mine. He did not look at my ankle nor was he distracted by others who happened along during that time.

Finally I spoke and asked if he could help me down to Base Camp. I promised to convert some of my earnings into Sherpa currency and pay him once we arrived.

"I can do that," he said quietly.

Neither of us moved. I sensed I was not supposed to.

When I could no longer stand staring into this man's eyes, I diverted my glance from his, looked up the slope and said what I really wanted was to be able to continue my climb.

"You can do that," he said quietly – just as before.

I tuned back to him and the look on my face must have shown him how confused I was.

"Climb or quit, you decide." He spoke without batting an eye and without changing his expression.

I looked at my ankle as if to encourage him to look and see what the problem was. He did not look.

I struggled to sit up and grimaced and moaned when my ankle moved. His expression did not change.

I stared at the Sherpa. Finally I said simply, "Climb."

He turned and walked away without saying a word.

A few minutes later the Sherpa returned carrying a forked stick. It was almost as tall as I was and it was as big around as my wrist. As he neared me he placed the fork under his shoulder and used the stick as a crutch.

As he handed it to me he said, "Rest tonight, slow tomorrow, faster the next day."

I thanked him and then, knowing that Sherpas only help for payment in their currency, I asked him how I could repay him.

"You did," he said.

I asked him how. How could I have paid him already? Did he steal something from me when I was not looking? I asked him what his currency was.

"Faith," he said.

I looked down at the crutch and as I did I asked him to explain what he meant by his answer. He did not respond and when I looked up he was gone.

It was a most remarkable day.

5

I heard a new sound today. And the path is becoming very crowded.

I think I may be nearing the top of Mount Majority. My quest is almost over.

I hear music from time to time. I hear the bustling sounds that happen whenever there are a lot of people around. And occasionally I see a cloud of dust up ahead. I must be nearing the place where the Majority live.

Tonight I looked down the slope and could barely see Base Camp. It is as distant a memory now as it is far away by foot.

My body has healed nicely and I am grateful for the experience of overcoming the fall. It gives me courage that I may be able to overcome other setbacks in the future. I never saw the Sherpa again, though I saw others.

My estimation is that it will only be a short time before I am on Mount Majority and enjoying all that it has to offer.

Some of the other climbers around me seem to have stopped. They are building their huts right where we are and beginning to settle in. I am amazed that they would come this far, get this close and then stop. Only a little more climbing and they would be at the top. It only takes a little more to have the best. Why quit now?

They could be at the highest point in the world if they would only press on a little while longer.

It will be difficult to sleep tonight because, as soon as to-morrow, I could reach my goal!

Still, I must rest.

6

Disappointment.

Mount Majority is a major disappointment. I have been here for some time now. In fact, I was here at my last journal entry; I just did not know it. The other climbers were building their huts because they knew they had arrived.

I had expected more, somehow.

It took a while for me to realize that this was all there is.

Everyone here has a similar hut. Some are slightly larger or smaller. Some have almost indistinguishable differences which one hut owner uses to say his hut his better than another's. Most people rise at the same time, follow the same routine and end their days with the same monotonous activities. Apparently the routine on the climb has become a part of their nature. Now they live each day just like the day before.

The sense of adventure that motivated them to begin the climb seems to have been replaced by a sense of melancholy and boredom.

Everyone here wears green garments made from the local plants. After a while they begin to yellow and eventually turn brown so they buy new green garments. People who are wearing yellow or, God forbid, brown garments are looked down upon by the green-wearers. It is a status symbol to be wearing new green, regardless of what type of person you are.

There are six types of people on Mount Majority. The largest percentage of them, in fact nearly all of them, is Workers. These are people who devote their lives every day to doing the work that needs to be done. Some Workers supervise other Workers, but they are still Workers themselves.

There are also Preparers. These are people who rise very early in the morning and prepare the Mount for Workers. Some prepare food, others make sure the paths are clear and still others work behind the scenes so that the infrastructure of the Mount functions properly. These people are rarely seen and do not normally mix with the others on Mount Majority. They are up before other people and by the time other people are beginning their day, the Preparers are completing theirs.

There are religious leaders, known as Shamans. Shamans are the people who understand the deeper truths of life and explain them to the Workers. The Workers seem to have little time and even less interest in learning the higher truths of life, so they leave it to the Shamans. Once a week or so, the Workers will sit with their Shaman and hear a teaching. Some benefit from the teaching, some do not.

Then there are the Practitioners. Whenever a Worker or anyone else is not well, they visit the Practitioner who gives them herbs and concoctions that are supposed to make them better. Some benefit from this, some do not.

Another type of person on Mount Majority is the Militiaman. Militiamen are in charge of keeping the peace and making sure Workers do not get out of line. While they can restrict what we want to do sometimes, overall, they are good to have around. They make Mount Majority a nicer place in which to live.

There are Teachers on Mount Majority. Teachers know that learning is never complete and education must continue for a lifetime. The primary reason for this, they say, is that people forget and have to be re-taught. They do not need to be taught anything that is radically new or different; they just need refresher courses. Some take advantage of this; some do not.

Every day is basically the same. As the Preparers begin moving about, a cloud of dust begins to rise from the roads. By the time most of the Workers begin their day, all are moving in the cloud and cannot see very far ahead.

The monotony of it all is disappointing; very disappointing. I had expected more.

7

Revelation!

This morning I could not sleep so I arose early – earlier than the Preparers. As I walked around the top of Mount Majority, I saw something off in the distance. It appeared to be another mountain, one that is higher than Mount Majority. Is it possible that there is another mountain – one that is better?

The only person I could find to ask at that time of morning was a Militiaman. I pointed to the mountain out in the distance and asked him what it was. He became agitated and began asking me a lot of questions. Who was I? Why did I want to know? What business was it of mine?

I was surprised at his reaction and even more surprised when he ~~asked~~ ordered me to go with him. We went to the militia station and soon a Teacher, a Practitioner and a Shaman joined him.

After asking me many questions and determining that I only been on Mount Majority a short while, they began to answer my questions.

What I had seen was Mount Achievement. It was, by their telling, a place that was uninhabitable. They went on to tell me that people had tried to go through the valley that lay between Mount Majority and Mount Achievement but only a few had returned.

Those who did manage to return claimed to have crossed the valley and climbed the mountain. They all came back insane.

The Practitioner explained. He said that the trauma they

*must have faced fighting the perils in the valley, known as
the Valley of Learning, would make many people go insane.
If they somehow survived the valley and actually climbed
the mount, they would contract "altitude sickness" which,
again, would make them insane.*

*In any case, they would come back delusional, babbling non-
sense about this or that. No one paid them any attention and
they were ignored or quietly put away, usually by their families.*

*The Teacher explained that since no scientific evidence was
available about Mount Achievement, it must be of little or
no use. If it had value, the Teacher explained, some scien-
tists would have explored and studied it.*

I asked why I had never heard of Mount Achievement before.

*The Teacher drew a picture and showed how Mount
Achievement was not visible from Base Camp. Mount Majority
blocked the view of Mount Achievement. Once on Mount
Majority, most people were content and fell into their daily
routines and never really noticed Mount Achievement.*

*Back in Base Camp so it was not considered necessary or
wise to confuse the young minds there with talk of the other
mount. Besides, the Teacher said, there was nothing beyond
Mount Achievement, so there was no use in exploring it.*

*Finally the Shaman spoke. He spoke with an authoritative
voice and with beautiful words. The Shaman explained that
if God had meant for man to be on Mount Achievement, He
would have said so in the Holy Books.*

*I asked other questions but rather than answers I heard,
"Well, that's just the way it is," and "Everybody knows that*

isn't so..." Some of my questions made them nervous and often they would look at each other before one would tell me not to think so much.

Although I was not convinced, I pretended to be and soon, they let me leave. On my way back to my hut, I stopped on the edge of a cliff and stared out at the beautiful moonlit Mount Achievement. It was still and quiet, a beautiful time of night.

I heard a noise below me. Something was moving on the hill below. I stared into the underbrush and then saw that it was a man coming up from the Valley of Learning. He climbed up to the cliff, right where I was standing, stood up and looked me in the eye.

It was the Sherpa who had helped me on my climb.

He had just come out of the valley as if it were a most common occurrence for him.

We stared at each other for a moment and he said, "Climb or quit, you decide."

With that, he was gone.

I resolved to climb Mount Achievement.

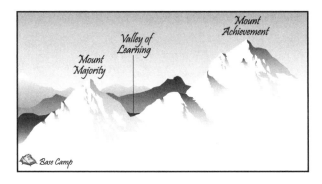

8

Today I began my climb of Mount Achievement.

I had asked as many questions as I thought I could without raising suspicion. All I know is that the Valley of Learning is a dangerous place. Some have told me that there are brambles in the valley that can entangle a person's feet until they cannot walk. Others have told about tiny insects that fly around, virtually unseen and bite anyone they find. The bites can make a person sick – or even cause death.

I do not know which to believe, so I will be prepared for both.

There would be no well-worn path this time like there was climbing Mount Majority. The only way I knew to begin was to go into the valley where I had seen the Sherpa come up.

I left before dawn and before the Preparers were out. It was my best chance for slipping out unseen. Only the Militiamen were roaming about. I thought I had made a clean escape until I edged myself over the ledge where I had seen the Sherpa pull himself up. My feet were already over the side when I heard the footsteps of a Militiaman.

I froze. Perhaps the shadows would keep him from seeing me. He kept walking right towards me – I knew I had been spotted. Then, remarkably, he stood right above me, his boot only inches from my hand. He could not see me!

The moon was bright enough and he was close enough for me to be able to read his nametag. His name was Ignorance and if he could, he would have prevented me from entering the Valley of Learning.

Once he walked away, I waited silently and then began the descent into the valley. As soon as I was down the hill and out of sight, I waited for the sun to come up and began my trek through the Valley of Learning.

This valley is not very deep. It is not nearly as deep as it appeared from the top of Mount Majority. After my first day here I have encountered some brambles but they have not been a problem. I just have to be careful to lift my foot higher when I take a step and make sure my toe is not stuck under a vine. I can see how people might get tripped up.

No insects yet.

The best part is the fruit. The fruit here is better than any on the climb to Mount Majority. It is more plentiful, probably because there are fewer people to eat it. And it is sweeter, it has more juice and it makes me feel like I have more energy.

As I rest for the evening, I can see Mount Majority and it is quite a distance away. I have made good time, I do not feel tired, but I will rest now and wait for the morning sunlight before continuing.

9

I know why it is called the Valley of Learning.

The first few days in the valley were not easy, but they were easier than now. The brambles are becoming thicker and denser. The brambles now have thorns on them. It is easier to trip now and I have fallen several times. Because of the thickness of the underbrush, the falls do not result in injury, only lost time and a few scratches from the thorns.

The insects I was warned about are real. I have been bitten many times but have not gotten sick. The insects only bite three or four hours after I have eaten. They do not come around while I am eating or when I sleep, so I am thankful for that.

Today I had to step across a small ravine. As I did, an insect buzzed my ear and I turned to swat it. Somehow, I managed to hopelessly entangle one foot in the brambles on the other side. I was straddling the ravine, swatting the insects and trying to free my foot all at the same time.

I realized that if I lost my balance, I would fall into the ravine. While it was not a large ravine, any fall would be disastrous and possibly fatal. For the first time I began to panic.

I felt my heart rate go up. I began to sweat profusely, more form nerves than from exertion. The first good thing that happened was that the insects mysteriously disappeared.

No amount of pulling or jerking was working. My foot was tightly ensnarled in the brambles. I was about to lose hope and yelled out, although I knew there was probably no one around to hear. That's when a Sherpa appeared.

Like the other Sherpas I had encountered, he simply stared at me. I asked him to help me free my foot, which by now was even more entangled. I thought he would reach down and pull away the brambles which I could not reach.

"I can do that," he said.

But he did not move. He just stared at me. He did not even look where my foot was entangled. Then he said, "Mind or muscle, you decide."

Somehow, I knew immediately what he meant. I could use my brain or my brawn. I could try to struggle my way out of this or I could try to reason my way out.

"Mind," I said. My muscles were not going to get me out of this one.

The Sherpa picked up his foot where I could see it. First he pointed his toe down and to the side, and then he twisted his foot clockwise, raised it slightly and then twisted it counter-clockwise. The Sherpa then pointed his toe upwards, twisted it clockwise again, pointed his toe downward and took a step.

I tried to repeat his movements with my foot, but my foot was still tangled. I looked at the Sherpa with a questioning expression. He simply repeated the same series of moves with his foot as he had done earlier.

It took four tries, but it worked. I was able to remember and mimic his gestures, free my foot and stand on the other side of the ravine beside the Sherpa.

Then I remembered that the Sherpas must be paid in their own currency.

"How do I repay you?" I asked. Then I remembered that the last Sherpa said currency was faith.

"You did," he said.

"You mean faith?" I asked.

The Sherpa shook his head and said, "Obedience."

I had worked up a thirst and turned to take out my water bottle. I held it out to offer the Sherpa the first drink, but he was gone.

Tonight I am wondering about obedience and obeying. I wonder what connection that has to faith. I have made camp in a clearing and as I thought about the events of the day, I wrote on the ground with my finger: "Obey Faith".

The Sherpa had challenged me to use my mind or my muscle. Faith is in the mind, not the muscles. I had obeyed faith and trusted thoughts over action.

Another thought came to me. Why are there no insects after I eat or when I sleep?

Maybe it's the fruit. Maybe the fruit repels these insects. After I eat, I smell like fruit. It is my essence. When I sleep, the fruit from my evening meal is all around me. But what about the mysterious way the insects disappeared when I was under stress? As I thought about it, I realized that under stress, I sweat. When I sweat whatever substances are in my body come out as perspiration.

Today I learned that whatever is in me can make me stronger while it repels what might harm me. This is an important lesson. I can use my mind, my learning, to replace some physical activities. I will use the essence instead of swatting insects.

10

I meet another Climber.

Today I began my ascent of Mount Achievement. I have learned many lessons from my trek through the Valley of Learning, too many to list here. Clearly the learning is vital for anyone who wants to achieve anything of lasting significance. What I have learned has become a part of my being – my essence. No one can teach the lessons to another; the lessons cannot be taught. One can only <u>learn</u> the lessons through education or, in my case, through the experiences I had in the valley.

The brambles are becoming scarce; perhaps it is the altitude. The insects have not been a problem since I learned how to deal with them.

It turns out that the valley actually rises and now, as I begin my climb up Mount Achievement, I look back at Mount Majority and it is not much higher than where I am right now. Soon I will be at a higher altitude than the highest point of Mount Majority. Maybe this is where I will need to watch for signs of altitude sickness the Practitioner warned me about.

The first indication that altitude sickness is real came today. I met another climber but he was walking back towards Mount Majority. He was a humble man, not the sort that would seem to go out on an adventure like this.

We stopped and talked for a long time. He spoke with great enthusiasm and energy. He told me that he had been to the top of Mount Achievement and it was grander than any-

thing he could have imagined. He told me about the people I would encounter there.

Then he said the most remarkable thing I had ever heard. He said there is another Mount beyond this one!

As soon as he saw the next Mount, he resolved to return to Mount Majority and tell everyone there the good news. He has family and friends on Mount Majority and he wants them to experience what he has.

We talked about the difficulties in crossing the Valley of Learning and how few people would make such a difficult trip. He was convinced that he could persuade many people to follow him. He, too, had met a Sherpa on his trip and now he felt he could teach the others what the Sherpa had taught him —the same lessons I had learned.

"But will they believe you?" I asked. "Will they just say you have altitude fever?"

He said he did not care what people thought of him. He only cared what he thought of others. And he thought he could help a lot of people.

After we parted company, I climbed for a while and then stopped for the evening. If what I had seen in the other Climber was altitude fever, I should also return to Mount Majority. I do not want to contract altitude sickness. I do not want to live my life on Mount Majority, either. So I will press on.

For the first time, I am wondering how many mounts there may be. If I reach the top of Mount Achievement and I find what the climber today said I would find, then there is a future. If not, maybe I will be insane. I do not know what is ahead, but I do know what is behind me. What I have seen is disappointing.

I believe there is something better. I have faith. I will obey faith.

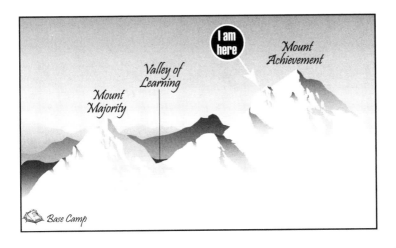

11

I knew when I had reached the top of Mount Achievement.

Unlike my unremarkable arrival on Mount Majority, I knew I had arrived.

I could tell by the people I met. There were only a few people there. Most were Teachers; the next largest group was Shamans; there were some Practitioners and one Militiaman. There were no Preparers and no Workers.

All of the people were dressed in bronze garments, which were very ornate but appeared to be uncomfortable. I was given a bronze garment and was surprised at how good it felt. It offered more protection than the green garments I had begun wearing on Mount Majority and it certainly looked better. It would also last a long time, maybe even a lifetime. I would no longer need to be so concerned about what I wore.

Off in the distance I could see, very clearly, another Mount. It was higher and more beautiful than Mount Achievement. There was also a valley separating the two Mounts.

Everyone was pleasant, agreeable and seemed interested in whatever I had to say. The day I arrived, a group of them greeted me and we immediately sat down to talk. There were several Teachers, Shamans, and Practitioners in our group and the one Militiaman joined us shortly after we began.

They told me that everyone there had achieved something significant in their life. Each had crossed through the

Valley of Learning and now possessed knowledge. The people who chose remain on Mount Achievement were the ones who valued knowledge and wanted to spend their lives delving into deeper and deeper truths. Whenever they uncovered a deeper truth, they would pass it on to a Climber who would carry it to the next Mount.

These people had no desire to travel to the next Mount themselves.

I had many questions and each was answered thoroughly and with great enthusiasm. These were people who enjoyed sharing knowledge.

Here is what I learned:

There is only one Militiaman here because few troublemakers ever make it this far. Most of his time is spent dwelling on smarter ways to keep the peace and to wage war when necessary.

There are no workers here because everyone pitches in and does whatever needs to be done. Most workers are only working to support other workers anyway. When there are fewer workers, there is less need for them.

On the higher Mounts, there are fewer and fewer people because few people strive to continue their climbs. There are many reasons for this. Some people are called to be teachers and want to go no farther than Base Camp, others no farther than Mount Majority, etc. Some people are afraid to try to move on. Still others believe the myths they have heard and resign themselves to lives of mediocrity.

The Next Mount is Mount Success and the valley between

these mounts is the Valley of Experience.

Each valley has two major hindrances, one is passive and the other is aggressive. Each must be overcome. The passive hindrances are ones we allow to hold us back. The aggressive hindrances attack us, usually in our areas of greatest weakness. In the Valley of Learning, the brambles were the passive hindrances and the insects were the aggressive hindrances.

At each successive valley, the hindrances become stronger. At each successive Mount, the rewards become greater.

There are a total of seven Mounts, and seven valleys. As they were described, I redrew my map:

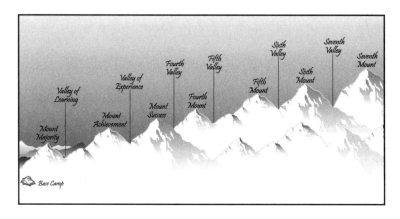

There are a total of seven Mounts but little is known about the seventh because no one has ever returned from it to tell others about it. I asked how they knew for sure that there was not certain death for those who ventured there and why anyone would risk it?

Each member of the group chuckled and looked at the others as if sharing an inside joke.

*The elder teacher spoke. She said, "The answer to your first question, 'How do we know for sure…' is **Faith**! The answer to your second question, 'Why would anyone try to go there…' is **Obedience**."*

This prompted me to ask about the Sherpas, the ones who had taught me about faith and obedience. Again the elder teacher in our group answered.

"Sherpas are guides. You will encounter them when you are ready and you will miss them when you are not ready." She continued, "They are everywhere, always."

I was thinking that I would continue my climb the next morning and was anxious to get some rest. We had talked for hours about what they had learned collectively. I stood to leave and thanked them for the bronze garment.

"You will need it for your climb tomorrow," said the Shaman.

I asked how he knew I would be leaving the next day. Each member of the group chuckled and looked at the others as if sharing an inside joke.

12

I spent time with the Teacher.

After leaving the group, I sat under a fruit tree to prepare for my journey tomorrow. The Teacher came over and we had a long, enlightening and important chat. She gave me twelve things to remember:

1. *Everyone is where he or she chooses to be. Consciously or subconsciously we all make choices that determine our place in the world. Some people are in Base Camp because they choose to spend their lives preparing others for the climb. Most are there because they chose to believe that one mistake holds a person back forever.*
2. *Anyone can change his or her choices at any time. The climb always begins in the mind. The climb is in the mind.*
3. *There are no extraordinary climbers. There are only those who appear to be extraordinary. Most appear extraordinary simply because they did not quit.*
4. *There are always Sherpas, or guides, around to help. Some people do not see them because they lack faith – the first payment of the Sherpas. Some will not do what the Sherpas tell them – out of fear, habits, laziness, etc. These are the ones who refuse to make the payment of obedience. (There are other payments Sherpas demand and I must learn those as I continue my climb. The Teacher knows them, but I must learn them, not be given them, she says.)*
5. *Once past Mount Majority, people move freely back and forth between Mounts. Some Climbers want to return and teach the people who have chosen to stay*

on lower Mounts. They are welcomed, not ridiculed or considered insane. (I will understand why this is so, the Teacher says, on the sixth Mount.)

6. Dwellers at lower levels are there for a reason – know what it is before taking their counsel. If they choose to remain there to teach others, take their advice. If they remain out of jealousy or fear or for any other lesser reason, we are wise to ignore their counsel. Some people substitute excuses for achievement.

7. True Climbers spend as much time in the valleys as on the Mounts, sometimes more. The Mount top experiences have their value, but it is the quest for the next level of understanding that makes a person complete.

8. Lessons learned in the valleys last a lifetime; Mount top experiences are but for a moment. A person cannot long survive on accolades but can live long and well on the lessons of adversity.

9. Each successive valley will have an important role in shaping the Climber; none must be skipped. The only way to skip a valley is to choose to stay on a lower Mount.

10. Each successive valley will be more difficult than the previous one. The climb does not become easier. The hindrances of the previous valleys must be overcome to enable the Climber to conquer the next one.

11. The seventh Mount is the most difficult to climb, it carries the greatest risk and the highest cost.

12. Every person is born with an innate longing to climb the seventh Mount.

I asked the Teacher if the Teachers on Mount Majority knew these twelve truths and she said, "On Mount Majority, the people do not know and they do not know that they *do not know." Then she continued, "Here, we do not know, but we know that we do not know."*

13

Today I began my climb to Mount Success and immediately turned it into the valley of failure.

Early this morning I began the next leg of my journey. It did not last long.

It occurred to me that I should ask what the hindrances are in the Valley of Experience, the valley between Mount Achievement and Mount Success. I knew the Militiaman would be awake and standing guard so I went to find him before leaving.

He was standing on a cliff looking out over the valley at Mount Success. As I approached, he turned and handed me a piece of paper. On the paper was written the names of each of the valleys between here and the seventh Mount as well as the passive and the aggressive hindrances in each.

When I asked how he knew I would want this, he chuckled.

The hindrances in the Valley of Experience that I am about to enter are swamps and snakes. The swamps are the passive hindrances; the snakes are the aggressive hindrances.

Perhaps the bronze garment will protect me from the snakes. Their fangs cannot penetrate bronze. Wearing Bronze in a swamp does not seem to be a good idea, though. We will see.

Just as before, I slipped out just before daylight. In retrospect this was foolish. I did not need to secretly leave as I had done before – the people on Mount Achievement would have helped me leave, not try to stop as the people on Mount Majority would have.

This proved to be my undoing.

When a person leaves Mount Achievement, they do not move down a slope as they do when leaving Mount Majority; they step out over a cliff. As soon as I moved my feet over the side, my weight pulled me down and I fell off the cliff. Had I waited until the sun was up, I would have been able to see this peril.

I bounced many times on my way down. I bounced off of ledges and bushes and small trees. Perhaps they helped to break my fall.

Now I am at the bottom of the cliff, scratched, bruised and bleeding. Both ankles are swollen. No crutch will serve me now.

After being here for some time, I began thinking. I cannot go back up the Mount. I cannot move forward. There are snakes in this valley.

I called for a Sherpa, I yelled for help many times. I am still all alone.

How do I obey faith in this situation?

Is this the end of my climb?

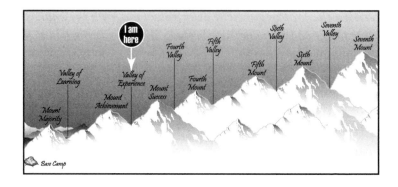

14

Two people came to help.

I had been here for several days and had managed to pull myself under a ledge. It would protect me from the weather but dragging myself there was difficult and painful. The sun was hot, my water was running low and the ledge afforded some shade.

A flash of light shot out from above me and I heard footsteps. Soon I heard voices. I called out for help. In a moment, two figures stood in front of me but I could not see them. There was a blinding glare, brighter than the sun, and all I could do was squint my eyes and stare in the general direction of the figures.

As my eyes acclimated to the bright light, I saw that there was a Sherpa and a Climber. The Climber was wearing an incredibly shiny garment. It was similar in design to the bronze garment I was wearing except for its color. The silver metal that was used to make it had been polished until it shone like a mirror.

When the sunlight reflected off of the garment, it shone so brightly that it distorted the size of the person wearing it. When I first saw the light and realized it was his clothing, I imagined that the wearer would be eight feet tall. When I was finally able to see him, he was no larger than I – maybe smaller.

The Climber spoke. "You look like you could use some help."

With that, the Climber and the Sherpa lifted me up and began carrying me by my arms. They sat me down by a stream, soaked some cloths in the water and wrapped my ankles. The water was very cold – almost freezing – so it stung when they applied the cloths.

The Sherpa stared into my eyes, as they always seem to do, as the Climber sat down beside me.

"I am from Mount Success," said the Climber, "and I'm just returning from a visit to Mount Achievement. When I first passed through Mount Achievement, I promised the Teacher I would return and give her a report of my climb up Mount Success. This Sherpa joined me yesterday."

The Climber wiped off a spot of dirt on his garment as he continued. "This is the garment given to those who climb Mount Success. You shall have one similar to this. But first you must cross the Valley of Experience and I think you are not off to such a good start."

He had said I would have a silver garment, so he must think that this setback of mine is not permanent. I asked him how I could best proceed.

The Climber looked at the Sherpa and then looked back at me and said, "The Sherpa and I will carry you."

I thought about the man's offer for a moment. I did not want to put these people out or slow down their climb. I was not sure if part of the process was having made the climb all by myself. Many thoughts raced through my mind as I tried to decide how best to proceed. I did not voice any of my thoughts.

I had decided that in order to be able to say I had earned my way up Mount Success, I would have to wait until my ankles had healed. But now that I was closer to the water, there was a greater danger from the snakes that live in the Valley of Experience.

While I was thinking, I looked up and saw the Sherpa staring into my eyes. "Be carried or wait, you decide," he said. Was he reading my mind?

There was something about the way he said it that made me realize that either decision was acceptable.

Not wanting to delay my journey, I said, "Be carried."

In a moment they had rigged some vines between two long branches and made a kind of stretcher. The Sherpa would walk in front, the Climber in the back and I could sit up on the webbing of vines. We were off.

As we walked, the Climber taught me the secrets of the Valley of Experience.

The snakes like to hide in the grass, so it is best to walk on rocks or in very short grass where they cannot hide.

The swamps are deceptive. Sometimes they are shallow and narrow. So walking across it not difficult and it can be a great shortcut. Others look shallow and small, but are actually larger and deeper. Many Climbers have gotten mired in these swamps and had to work their way back out. It cost a lot of time and took a lot of energy.

On one occasion, the Sherpa turned and began walking into some tall grass, the kind that the snakes prefer.

Straight ahead was what appeared to be a meadow with al-most no grass. I asked the Sherpa why he chose the tall grass and the man in silver answered.

"Straight ahead is one of the deadliest swamps. It looks so easy and alluring. It is not only deep and slippery, it is filled with the most venomous snakes of all."

Day after day we repeated this process. They carried me, they taught me how to recognize the different snakes and how to identify the worst swamps. On one occasion, I saw a large log across one of the swamps and pointed it out to the Sherpa. Walking across the log would have been faster than walking around the swamp. The Sherpa acted as if he had not heard me. As we passed by the swamp, the log rolled over and slithered below the surface. It turned out to be one of the largest snakes I had ever seen. It appeared as an asset; it was a snake. Now I know how even even the largest snakes – the ones that should be obvious to us, can fool Climbers.

After about a week, I began walking part of the day and by the end of another week, we discarded the stretcher. That is the same day we began our ascent up Mount Success.

The climb was somewhat more difficult than the previous ones; it was not just another climb. It had new hindrances, as had the others, in addition to the hindrances of the previous climbs. I have learned to move through the older hindrances. The brambles and insects are not a problem for me now.

It bothered me that I had not earned my way here. I was also puzzled by the idea that I had spent my time in the Valley of Experience learning from the Sherpa and the Climber in silver. Maybe this was supposed to be the Valley of Learning, not the Valley of Experience.

Tonight, as we stopped to make camp on the slope leading up to Mount Success, I asked my two companions about this.

Neither spoke for a moment. Finally the Sherpa said, "Learning is experience; experience is learning. You decide."

There is more than one way to learn just as there are many ways to experience the different aspects of the climb.

It is acceptable to accept help

.

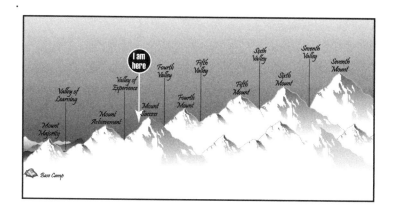

15

I cannot stop at Mount Success.

As the Climber in the silver garment had told me, as soon as I reached the summit of Mount Success, I was given a silver garment. It takes some getting used to. It is not as heavy as the bronze one I had been wearing. I am more agile with this one. Perhaps I will need the greater agility later.

As soon as we arrived, the Climber in Silver and the Sherpa continued on their way. I had not paid the Sherpa and he had done more for me than any of the others by carrying me most of the way through the Valley of Experience.

I ran and caught up with the Sherpa and asked what I owed him and, as before, he said I had already paid him. When I asked how, he did not say "Faith" or "Obedience", he said, "Trust". Yet another Sherpa currency.

I will have to give that some thought.

There are fewer people on Mount Success than there were on Mount Achievement. There are fewer types of people on Mount Success.

There are no Militiamen here.

Everyone here seems more animated and more positive. There are lively discussions going on wherever I turn. This morning I joined in a debate about the value of Sherpas and what their role is supposed to be for us Climbers. I was surprised to hear how many different opinions there are –

all from people who have climbed Mount Success.

Being on the same Mount does not mean that we think alike.

Then I sat and listened to an older gentleman talk about the restorative powers of the body. His position was that every physical ailment or injury could be overcome though the use of the mind. He was well into his dialog before I realized that he is one of only a few Practitioners here. Apparently, most of the Climbers who have reached Mount Success have learned somewhere along the way that Practitioners are not as necessary as they were at lower altitudes.

Still, there are a few that call on the services of the Practitioners – some quite often.

Being on the same Mount does not mean that we all act alike.

After the experience with the Practitioner, I saw a large group of people, all clad in silver garments, who were sitting and standing, listening to someone. As I neared the group, it seemed like they must have built a bon fire because there was an amber glow emanating from the center.

The glow turned out to be the speaker. It was another Climber, but she was wearing a brilliant gold garment. It radiated like the silver ones we were all wearing but it was a stronger, more powerful glow.

She talked about the next valley, the Valley of Risk and what we could expect as we continued our journeys there. She had returned from the next mount, Mount Significance, to teach anyone who wanted to learn what to expect on the next leg of the climb.

Someone had taught her, she said, and now she was repaying the favor. Actually, she called it a "debt".

In the Valley of Risk, there are brambles, insects, snakes and swamps and there are also tigers and quicksand. This will be the most perilous valley yet. The tigers are the new aggressive hindrances and the quicksand is the new passive hindrance.

I can tell that some of the Climbers who are listening to her will not make the journey. It is just too great a challenge. Besides, being on Mount Success is pretty incredible. The view here is awesome. There are great people here. Everyone is willing to teach and everyone is willing to listen to whatever ideas I have. I can see why some would choose to stay here. I am tempted to stay.

The Climbers on Mount Majority don't know and they don't know that they don't know. The Climbers on Mount Achievement don't know and they know they don't know.

Here on Mount Success, we know.

It is a wonderful place to be: mentally, physically and spiritually.

The Climber in gold says she has mastered the Valley of Risk and will soon return to Mount Significance. There must be a reason why. What is out there that is better than this?

It occurs to me that the Climbers learn something new as

they cross each Valley and climb each Mount. Each Climber also develops their own version of the skills they will need as they continue their climb.

The Climber in gold is confident that she can make her way back through the Valley of Risk to Mount Significance. Perhaps I will travel with her since I have learned the value of having other Climbers around me.

I am truly enjoying the time here, but I cannot stay on Mount Success.

16

The Valley of Risk may be more than I can handle.

The Climber in gold announced when she would begin her return to Mount Significance. Several of us joined her. The climb would be so much better this time, I thought, because there would be camaraderie among the fellow Climbers and we would have the benefit of an experienced Climber with us.

It did not turn out that way.

We had only been in the Valley of Risk for a few hours when we noticed that the Climber in gold was outpacing us. She was so far ahead of us that at times we lost sight of her. One of the other Climbers yelled at her and asked her to wait for us. She yelled back that her slowing down would not benefit any of us.

We were discussing what she must have meant by her comment when the first tiger appeared. It seemed to come from out of nowhere. It leapt into the midst of us and we all ran.

As I ran I felt my heart racing. My breath became hot and labored. My chest was burning. I surprised myself at how quickly I could dance through the brambles. When I saw the grass ahead make the unmistakable movement that indicated there was a snake in my path, I instinctively turned – always in the right direction.

When I neared a swamp I could actually smell it. My mind would race as my eyes scanned all around and without hesitation I would once again alter my course.

From somewhere deep inside of me, I was functioning without thinking. My actions and reactions were more a matter of reflex than anything else. I learned to trust my instincts. I learned to trust my physical abilities as I leapt over logs, stones and even ravines. I learned to trust my intuition about what was happening. I learned to trust my judgment. I learned to trust.

Trust. That is what the last Sherpa had taken as payment.

I had not looked back since I began running. It was like a nightmare. I knew there was a predator behind me. I knew other people were at risk. I had not stayed to fight; I had taken flight. It was every man for himself.

The whole idea of climbing with others had disappeared the first time a peril appeared.

When I could run no more, I slowed to a walk and dared to look back. All was still and quiet.

I found a clearing where no predator could sneak up on me. I climbed up on a boulder there and sat down to rest. After a while I saw some rustling in the brush and stood to get a better view. I was not nervous or afraid. Instinctively I knew there was no danger.

Two of the other Climbers walked into the clearing, saw me and waved.

They joined me on the boulder and we talked quietly. We did not want our voices to carry far enough to attract the attention of another tiger. We wondered what had happened to the other Climbers and talked about our options.

The other two Climbers asked how I had managed to run so much faster and farther than they had. I did not know. It was just instinct.

The sun was about to go down so we decided to camp on the boulder for the night. It would not be as comfortable as the grass but it would be safer. Insects were beginning to bother us so we decided to go and find some fruit and then return to the boulder for the night.

The three of us walked into the tree line searching for fruit. It took a while but we found some small fruit on a young tree. It was not much but it might be enough.

As we walked back towards the boulder in the clearing, one of the Climbers stopped and pointed. Across a sandy field was a huge tree that was drooping with some of the biggest, most beautiful fruit we had seen. Even from a distance we could smell the sweet fragrance of the luscious fruit. The sight and smell of the fruit tree seemed too good to be true.

The Climber who had spotted the fruit took off running towards the tree and as he ran, the ground seemed to swallow him. In a moment he was mired in the sand up to his waist. He turned to make his way back to where we were standing and as he did, he sank even further into the sand.

He struggled with all of his might and that only seemed to make his situation worse. We began walking slowly and carefully towards him. Soon, the sand was up to his chin. After one final struggle, we heard an awful, muffled scream and he was gone.

The remaining Climber and I stood and stared at the sand as it became still. It looked so innocent to have been so sinister.

Without speaking, we slowly turned and began walking back towards the boulder.

Our silver garments began looking like gold ones as the setting sun reflected off of them. Everything seemed surreal. How could someone come so far only to suffer a horrible and swift end to their climb?

The other Climber was probably having similar thoughts as we walked towards the clearing. We began eating the fruit. We certainly had no appetite after what we had just witnessed but we knew the importance of keeping the insects away.

Then, suddenly, without any sound, another tiger landed right between the other Climber and me. Before I knew what was happening the tiger had bared his fangs and leapt right towards my face.

Without thinking, I swiftly raised my arm to protect my face and did so just in time to hit the tiger on the bottom of his jaw. The sound of the metal on my arm connecting with the animal's jawbone is one I will not forget. The tiger's claws managed to put three parallel scratches on the back of my hand. The animal did a back flip and crumpled on the ground.

Again, without thinking, I kicked the tiger's head. The vicious animal let out a howl and then lay silent, not breathing.

My heart was beating so loudly that I assumed the other Climber could hear it. He had not moved from the place or even the position where he had been when the animal first appeared.

Why had he not reacted?

As I think about it, I believe it all happened too fast for him to react. The danger presented itself, I instinctively reacted and it was over.

I fell to the ground as I kept my eye on the tiger.

My mind was racing. Trusting my instincts had paid off again. Now I knew I could also trust my garments. They had been given to me for a reason.

We spent the night on the boulder with no further incidents.

The next day we set out once again for Mount Significance. We were more sober now. The events of the previous day combined with all we had learned gave us a new sense of purpose and an appreciation for the climb.

We talked as we made our way through the brambles, around the swamps, avoiding snakes and watching out for tigers. Our climb continued like that for several more weeks.

We encountered tigers occasionally. The first few were dealt with the same way: I hit them as hard as I could with either my arm covering or my leg covering and that was the end of their threats. Soon my climbing partner was also confidently dealing with the tigers in a similar manner.

What was interesting is that after a while, we showed no fear as the tigers appeared and they simply turned and moved away. I suppose they went looking for other prey.

We did manage to wander into a few of the quicksand pits.

However, we were alert and as soon as we saw we were entering one, we turned and pulled each other out. We never allowed ourselves to risk going through one, even if it appeared to be narrow enough to reach across.

On the third day of the seventh week, something happened that I am still trying to figure out. We were climbing, making good time when we came upon a tiger. Unlike the others, this one was lying across the path on which we were walking. It was quietly grooming itself. It looked up at us, paused, and then went back to its grooming. We seemed to be of little interest to the tiger.

The other Climber and I stopped and took a break. We drank some water and kept our eye on the tiger. The other Climber moved a few feet away from me and leaned up against a rock.

The tiger stood up slowly and stretched by putting both paws out in front of itself and bowing down to the ground. Then the animal turned and faced us and began walking very slowly towards us. It was purring. I had never spent as much time observing these animals. They are magnificent creatures.

As the animal came nearer, I stiffened and slowly drew back my arm, ready to swing it in the direction of the tiger if it came close enough. The animal was majestic, beautiful – even mesmerizing. But it was still a tiger. The animal slowly walked over to the other Climber

I was surprised to see that the other Climber was smiling at the sight of this big animal walking towards him. The tiger seemed docile enough but it was still a tiger. Then, unbelievably, the tiger began rubbing itself on the other

Climber's leg. The purring continued. I could see the muscles in the other Climber relax as the animal seemed to be communicating with him.

Had we finally mastered the beasts? Did they know that we were their masters?

The other Climber gently reached down and stroked the hair on the back of the tiger's head. The tiger stretched its head upwards seeming to enjoy the feeling.

Then, in one sudden and sure move, the tiger lurched, grabbed the other Climber by the throat and dragged him off into the brush. The other Climber's body was twitching and struggling but I did not hear a sound.

The Valley of Risk may be too much for me.

Each of the other two Climbers had been intelligent, experienced Climbers. They had each conquered Mounts Achievement and Success and were on their way to Significance. Just like me.

The journey had become more perilous. I am no smarter and no more experienced than they. How is it that I am still on the climb? Is the climb really a matter of luck?

The hindrances are everywhere now. Brambles at every step, it seems, except where there is a swamp or quicksand. Still I manage to find enough sure footing to continue my climb. Insects, snakes and tigers outnumber me. Yet I remain.

As I approach Mount Significance, I am questioning whether the journey is worth the cost.

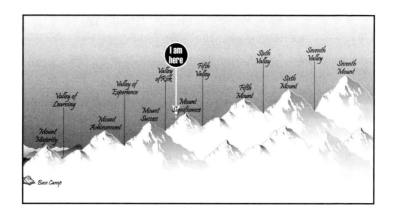

17

Mount Significance is where I will stop.

I arrived on Mount Significance several days ago. I was given my gold garment. It is just fine.

As soon as I could, I found an empty hut and laid down to rest. I am told that I slept for three days.

The climb up Mount Significance was the toughest yet. On the other Mounts, there were no brambles after a while. Here the brambles continued all the way to the top. On the other Mounts, there are no insects or snakes or tigers. The slope up to Mount Significance was populated with all of them. In addition to those hindrances, I also had to contend with the climb, which was steeper than I remember the other slopes being.

I will end my climb here.

Since the climb only becomes more difficult, I think I have reached my limit.

I admire those brave Climbers who have returned back through the Valley of Risk to teach and encourage the Climbers back on Mount Success. I admire them more than ever. I now understand and appreciate what they have done. Perhaps when I am rested, I will make a trek back to one or more of the other Mounts and encourage the Climbers I find there.

Still, I have the highest admiration for the Climbers who have continued on from here to Mount Wisdom. Those

Climbers, after all, have had to pass through the Valley of Failure. While Mount Wisdom is somewhat appealing to me, having to cross the Valley of Failure cancels out any desire I might have had.

After waking from my long sleep, I spent the next few days mostly by myself. That is easier to do since there are fewer people here. Mount Significance is larger than any of the other Mounts I have been on. It is large enough for everyone to have plenty of room. Still, only a few have taken the Valleys of Learning, Experience and Risk in order to be here.

There is a steady stream of Climbers coming and going between this Mount and the ones on either side. Nearly all are Sherpas.

Occasionally there is a Climber like me. I can tell by the scars on their ankles from walking through the brambles. Many have the unmistakable welts from insect bites or the distinctive marks from a tiger's paw. They all seem to have the same aura about them as well. It's a combination of fatigue and determination.

Still, when I see Climbers coming and going, I assume they are Sherpas. There are more of them here than I saw on my climb below.

Almost everyone here is a Teacher. Some of the Teachers were once something else.

Some were Practitioners who advanced beyond the place where they were needed, and so they became Teachers. They came to understand the incredible healing and restorative qualities that are innate within each of us. And so they teach this new understanding as a method of healing. They are still Practitioners, in a way.

Some of the Teachers were once Shamans who found themselves surrounded by people who had taken the time to learn all they could from every Shaman they encountered. As a result, they were Shamans among Shamans. Now they teach as they are able to better understand the truths of life.

Some were workers who somehow sensed, back on Mount majority, that they were destined for more. They evolved, first as low-ranking Militiamen, Under-Shamans or Para-Practitioners until they finally reached Mount Significance. And now they understand and teach the truth that anyone can make it to Significance.

What all of these people have is common is understanding.

While on Mount Majority, we did not know and did not know that we did not know. On Mount Achievement, we knew that we did not know. On Mount Success, we knew and we knew that we knew.

Now, we understand.

It is a deeper level of living than anyone on a lower Mount could possibly conceive.

I mostly sit and listen. I am tired, I do not plan to move on any farther and so I feel I have little to contribute. I feel somewhat out of place since most of the Climbers on this Mount are very animated. They laugh a lot and they encourage each other often.

In a discussion, the topic of Sherpas came up. Many opinions were offered about their purpose and their heritage.

The elder Teacher listened to this discussion and, when there was a lull in the chatter, he spoke and said, "Guides."

Everyone turned and looked at him as he continued speaking. "They are Guides. Some say Angels. Same thing."

He paused while we absorbed what he was saying. "The Creator sends them back from the Seventh Mount. They are available to all."

Someone asked the elder Teacher why there were more here on Mount Significance than on any other Mount. After all, it would seem, the Climbers on the lower Mounts needed them more than we did.

His answer was revealing.

"More Sherpas or more Climbers able to see them?" he asked. Then he said, "You decide."

By now I have been in many discussions. I have spent time around the elder Teacher. I feel my level of understanding is rising. Yet, the more I understand, the more I find that I want to understand. Understanding becomes its own insatiable thirst.

I sat alone this evening on the side of Mount Significance that faces Mount Wisdom. The Mount stood silent out in the distance. The valley of Failure that stretched out between me and the Mount seemed quiet and peaceful. But I knew it held its own ominous hindrances.

I was aware that someone was coming towards me. I turned in time to see the elder Teacher sit down beside me.

For a while, we just sat, enjoying the view and the quiet.

Then I asked, "Will the hunger for understanding ever be satisfied?"

The elder Teacher nodded.

"How?" I asked.

The elder Teacher looked towards the distant Mount and said, "Wisdom."

I knew what he meant. The desire that burned within me would never be satisfied with anything less than Wisdom. How could he know this? Had he been to Mount Wisdom and returned to teach us? Had he been even farther?

I had to ask him.

"Are you a Sherpa?"

He continued to look at the Mount as it disappeared into the night.

"You decide," he said.

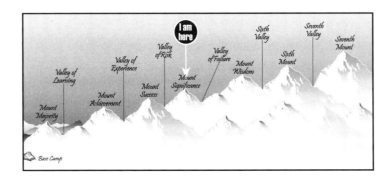

18

I decide to leave Mount Significance and I am more scared than ever before .

My gold garment is as comfortable for me now as any other has been. I enjoy spending time with each of the people here, but the longing in my spirit will not go away and so I know I must press on to Mount Wisdom.

I have intentionally delayed hoping that a Climber from Mount Wisdom would come through and I could follow them back. If not, at least I could learn from them what I could expect in the Valley of Failure.

When I first arrived, there were the occasional Climbers that passed through here. But since I have decided to move on, the only ones passing through are Sherpas. I have learned not to try and follow a Sherpa. They can – and will – travel faster than any Climber. They seem to be unaffected by the hindrances.

My hunger to be on Mount Wisdom becomes greater with each passing day.
I know that I will face all of the hindrances that I have encountered in the past as I move forward. And, I know that there will be new challenges as well. There is a part of me that is anxious to begin and there is another part of me that only feels dread at the thought of continuing the climb.

It occurred to me that perhaps it would help if I went back to visit Mount Success. Maybe seeing where I had been in the past would help me appreciate where I am now. And it could be that going back through the Valley of Risk, know-

ing what I know now, would somehow boost my confidence.

There is also a part of me that wants to go back and encourage others who have not made it this far. I could warn them about the new dangers in the Valley and I could tell them about the view from the top of Mount Significance. If I could just inspire one person to make climb, a person who would otherwise have stayed on Mount Success, then the return trip would be worthwhile.

I made the descent and was surprised at how easy it was. The terrain in the Valley was familiar. The hindrances were there but were easily dealt with. When I went through the Valley the first time, I was totally focused on the steps I was taking. I was trying to be careful to watch for the hindrances. On this return trip I was able to look around and see things I had missed the first time through.

In only a couple of days I was walking up Mount Success. I say walking because it did not feel like much of a climb. The conditioning of my body and the courage in my spirit combined to make passing back through previous valleys much easier.

Once on top, the Climbers there immediately surrounded me. I had forgotten for a moment that my garment was different, but when I saw the gold of my garment reflecting off of their silver garments, I remembered.

This was an opportunity for me to teach the Climbers at a lower Mount. More importantly, it was an opportunity for me to come face-to-face with the level of success I had attained. Not only had I made the physical journey back, I was also being reminded of where I had been mentally and spiritually.

The other Climbers on Mount Success probably thought that this was a generous gesture on my part. That is what I had thought when I had met the Climber from Mount Significance during my stay on Mount Success. In fact, this was as much for me as it was for them.

Among those who gathered around me were some familiar faces: Climbers who were on Mount Success when I was there. How long would they delay making their climb?

After a few days on Mount Success I returned to Mount Significance. There was a new feeling of pride inside of me. I had been a teacher and, in many ways, a servant. As I made my way back through the Valley of Risk, I felt better about myself.

That was several weeks ago. Now it is time to make my way to the Fifth Mount, Mount Wisdom, on the other side of the Valley of Failure.

Last night I spent a long time with the elder Teacher. I am convinced he is some form of a Sherpa. He does not say much but when he does speak, whatever he says has great value. He says that I will have to face the greatest hindrances yet in the Valley of Failure. The way he says it, I become frightened and excited all at once. The feeling is not unlike what soldiers must feel prior to going into battle.

When I asked him specifically what the hindrances were, he did not answer.

I asked him why this was called the Valley of Failure when so many Climbers had failed in previous valleys, especially the last one, the Valley of Risk.

"First you recognize," he said, "and then you experience."

He continued, "The first valley was the Valley of Learning, but you thought you had learned in Base Camp. The second valley was the Valley of Experience, but you thought you had your experience in the Valley of Learning. So it goes. First you recognize the matter, then you experience it."

I thought for a minute and then asked, "So now I am really about to experience failure?"

"You decide," he said.

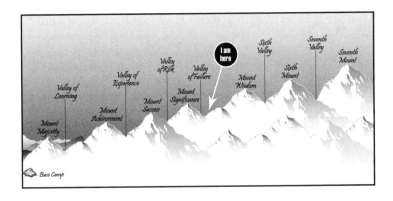

19

At the base of Mount Wisdom I make a decision.

*I have been resting here at the base for days. I am ex-
hausted. The journey through the last valley was so severe
that I did not stop to make any entries in my journal.*

*The Valley of Failure is the most appropriately named Val-
ley of them all. There are more ways to fail there than there
are to succeed. Many more.*

*Still, if I had to give it another name, I would call it the Val-
ley of Fire. It was a relentless trial by fire.*

*The heat was almost unbearable. My gold garment
reflected much of the heat away from my body, but at times
even it was hot to the touch in places. I did not dare remove
it because I understood the value of the protection it
offered.*

*Sleeping at night was difficult and fretful because of the
heat. The fruit in the Valley was plentiful but it was warm
and not as satisfying as the fruit in previous Valleys had
been.*

*Much of this Valley has been burned. There must have been
huge forest fires here. The deeper I went into the valley, the
less often I saw anything green. Almost everywhere I
stepped the ground was black and covered in soot or ash.
This Valley is as desolate a place as I can imagine.*

*From the very first day, I had my share of encounters with
brambles, insects, tigers, snakes and all of the other*

hindrances I have learned to conquer. The difference was that the brambles were mostly brown. While they looked dried out, they were still tough and capable of tripping even the most experienced Climber and the thorns were just as painful. The snakes and tigers were covered in soot and ashes and often hid under debris that was the same color. They were more difficult to identify.

This valley was the least hospitable place I had ever been.

On the third day, I found myself between two cliffs that formed a very narrow pass where two mountains met.

I considered my options. I could walk through the pass, which was obviously the easiest way. My experience told me that the easy way is usually not the best way. I could scale the cliffs but there was the obvious risk of falling. Going around either of the mountains would take a very long time and there was no assurance of what I would find if I tried that approach.

I stood and studied the ground that I would have to cross if I chose the easy way through the pass. I had learned that there are times when it is best to just stop and look and consider the route I am about to take. Even with all of my experience, I have learned to move cautiously at times – especially when covering new ground.

My patience paid off. As I stared at what appeared to be solid ground, at one point it moved. It did not move significantly, just enough to let me know that it was not solid. I recognized the movement.

This was a swamp. I considered the idea that it might be a different type of quicksand, but concluded that it was a *swamp. This would be the first swamp I had encountered in the Valley of Failure, or so I surmised. It did not look like the swamps in other valleys; it looked like solid earth. It was ringed with what I thought must have been a fungus or plant of some kind that was a brilliant yellow-orange.*

On the other side of the swamp were some huge boulders.

I watched the swamp long enough to conclude that it was too wide to jump across but not too wide to wade or swim across, as long as it was not too deep. Because this swamp looked and behaved differently from the others I had encountered, I decided to take no chances. I could not know what lived in the swamp, so even a short time in it could prove to be disastrous.

I looked around and found a tall tree, one that would be long enough to stretch across the swamp to the other side. I tried to fell the tree by climbing up it and rocking back and forth. The tree would not bend enough to break, so I climbed down.

I found another tree, about as tall, but smaller in diameter. It would not be as strong, but strong enough, I thought. After some effort I managed to bend it to the ground. Some jumping on the bent trunk caused the tree to eventually split and I was able to twist it free.

I drug the tree back to the swamp. On the side of the swamp where I was, I stood the tree on end and allowed it to drop to the other side where it rested on one of the boulders. Then I lifted the trunk of the tree as high as I could and placed it on one of the outcroppings of the cliff.

Using a hand-over-hand technique, I would be able to cross the swamp without having my feet touch the water. If there was any danger, I surmised, it would have to be from a creature that could jump up out of the swamp. I had not seen anything break the surface of the water, so I felt I had found the best solution. I was pleased with my cleverness.

I pulled myself up on the tree trunk and realized I had not accounted for the weight of the gold garment. The tree trunk creaked, but it held. I bounced up and down a few times and the tree trunk continued to hold.

I began crossing the swamp. I started out slowly and quickly gained confidence. My feet were at least a foot from the surface of the swamp. I was sweating profusely from the heat and from the exertion. Sometimes the sweat would be so thick in my eyes that I could not see clearly.

I was more than half way across when it happened.

Somehow, I managed to roll the tree trunk just enough for the base to roll off the outcropping and land on the ground. When it did, my feet went into the swamp. That is when I learned that it was not a swamp; it was a lava pit.

Both of my feet were badly burned before I could jerk them back up. I began scrambling furiously to reach the boulders. My feet were out in front of me; my hands were slippery from the sweat. I could hardly see. All I can remember is scrambling for the other side.

I knew what would happen if I lost my grip.

In my haste I managed to ram my scorched feet into the boulder. I let out a howl that reverberated off of the cliff walls.

I reached the point where the tree met the bounder. My feet were sticking out off to one side and I was trying to determine how I could lift myself up on the rock. All of my weight and the weight of my garment were suspended in the air by my grip on the tree trunk. My eyes were watering even more, probably as much from tears as sweat.

I twisted and managed to swing one leg up on the boulder. I hung in that position, too tired to move any more, even as I felt my grip on the log slipping. I was moaning.

I felt a hand on the ankle of my foot that was on the boulder. Then I felt another hand grip my dangling ankle. Soon I was on top of the rock. I was in a lot of pain.

Instinctively I knew that a Sherpa had helped me. I was in too much pain to speak to him, even to say thank you.

For the first time, I knew what the other Climbers who had failed must have felt. I had found the aggressive hindrance of the Valley of Risk, and it had defeated me.

"Not aggressive; passive. Not defeated." The voice came from above me. The Sherpa was standing above me and somehow knew my thoughts.

There was no "You decide" tacked on to this response. This was different.

My head was spinning. The lava pit was the passive hindrance. Despite the severe burns on my feet, the Sherpa believed there was hope. What was the aggressive hindrance in this valley? How would I be able to continue?

I asked the Sherpa, "How?"

There was no answer. He was gone.

I drug myself over to the edge of the boulder and looked down at the lava pit. As I studied it, I realized that the brilliant yellow-orange ring around the pit was actually melted gold. I wondered how many Climbers had reached this point only to contribute to the ring around the pit.

The Sherpa returned with an armload of what appeared to be palm branches and both hands full of white clay. He knelt down at my feet and used one hand full of the white clay to cover the bottom of one foot. It did not hurt, as I thought it would. Instead it actually felt cool.

Then the Sherpa fashioned a kind of woven boot out of the palm leaves. The boot held the clay tightly to my foot.

Then the Sherpa sat down a few feet away.

I knew what to do. I took the other batch of clay and the palm leaves and fashioned a boot for my other foot. I diligently copied what he had done.

This is the way the Sherpas teach.

With that, the Sherpa stood, reached out his hand and helped me to my feet. Amazingly, I could stand.

The Sherpa headed towards Mount Significance, which was the opposite of the way I was going. I let him go. I could not have kept up with him anyway.

The weeks in the Valley of Failure were the toughest ones yet. My feet are better, but still tender. There are ugly scars on them.

The problem is that I have not found out what the aggressive hindrance is here. That can only mean one thing: it is somewhere on the slope leading up to Mount Wisdom. After several days here at the base of the Mount, I have been debating in my mind whether I will continue my climb and risk facing the other hindrance or return to Mount Significance.

When I first arrived at Mount Significance I thought I would end my climb there. Maybe that was the right decision. Looking back, being on Significance, being around those incredible people, returning to lower Mounts from time to time to teach – that was a great life. Few people have reached that place in their lives. Why would I want to risk losing it all just to go to the next level?

So, after considering all of my options and arguing in my mind for these past few days, I have decided to continue my climb. I understand the risk. I understand the potential costs. I understand this could be my last entry.

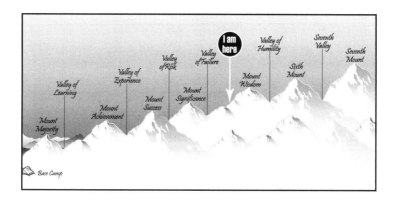

20

I underestimated the cost of reaching the Fifth Mount.

Mount Wisdom was steeper than any of the previous Mounts. I was having greater difficulty climbing because of that. By now my feet were covered in scar tissue and calluses and that actually helped me make the climb. My feet are tougher now than ever.

I was on the lookout for the aggressive hindrance of the Valley of Failure. As steep as the slope had become, I knew there could be no swamps, quicksand or lava pools there.

As I continued my climb, I began to notice recesses in the side of Mount Wisdom. The higher I climbed, the larger the recesses became. In fact, on the fourth day of the ascent I was able to crawl into one of the recesses for my night's rest. It was the first time I had felt ~~cool~~ less hot since I entered the Valley.

On the seventh day of my ascent up Mount Wisdom I came face to face with the aggressive hindrance of the valley. A large lizard-like creature came out of one of the recesses. He was slightly larger than I am and had a bright red tongue that flicked out as it walked.

The creature was ahead of me and, therefore, higher than I was on the Mount. I had just gripped a tree and was about to pull myself up but I decided I should wait and see what the creature would do.

As I watched, the huge lizard turned, saw me, flared its eyes and nostrils and stood as tall as it could on its short legs.

The next thing I knew, I felt a searing heat on my lips. I raised my hand towards my mouth just in time for my arm to deflect the lizard's tongue as it lashed out towards my eyes.

My mouth was burning and the pain was so severe that I could not even scream. I realize now that this creature was a dragon and its first instinct was to keep its prey from calling for the help of a Sherpa or another Climber. Its second strike was supposed to have blinded me. My instincts had paid off again but the dragon was only beginning.

It began moving towards me and I was amazed at how easily it maneuvered itself on the steep slope. It never took its eyes off of me; it just continued to stalk me, lashing out its tongue at irregular intervals.

The dragon managed to hit me with its tongue on the back of my hand and immediately a large welt appeared. Another time it began repeatedly lashing out at my feet, trying to trip me up. I was able to dance around these lashes and none ever burned my feet.

I was moving down the Mount now, watching the dragon, taking quick glimpses behind me to see where I was going and then watching the dragon again.

I was no match for the dragon.

Finally, I stopped backing away. Instinctively I knew that I was not supposed to be giving up the ground I had covered. I was to face down this creature.

Keeping my arm in front of me with my hand balled up into a tight fist, I began moving towards the dragon. It began lashing its tongue at me faster and faster. It began to hiss. It also began to back away.

I began taking quick glimpses up the Mount instead of down behind me. I saw a way to climb around the dragon's recess. After I had climbed back up to about where I had encountered the dragon, I began moving to the side of the dragon's recess.

The dragon continued to lash out at me but it was a more timid act than it had been. Once I was above its recess, the dragon simply walked back inside of it.

I climbed for another hour or so and then took a break. I needed some of the clay the Sherpa had given me to treat the burns on my mouth and hands. The only place I knew to find the clay was back down deep in the valley.

As I sat on the side of the Mount, I thought back to the conversations I'd had with some of the Practitioners. The Practitioners on the lower Mounts had talked about the restorative capabilities of the body. The body is controlled by the mind. The body responds to what the mind tells it.

I began to concentrate on how cool and soothing the clay had felt when the Sherpa applied it to my feet. I imagined how it would feel on my lips. I imagined how it would feel on my hand.

I concentrated on these thoughts over and over for some time and then realized that the burning on my mouth was not as bad as it had been. My hand did not ache as much as it had. The more I concentrated on the healing properties of the clay, the better I felt. The welts on the back of my hand did not change, but the pain from the burning lessened significantly.

It took several weeks for me to complete my climb up Mount Wisdom. During that time I encountered several more dragons, some larger, some smaller than the first one. On each occasion, I immediately covered my face and began moving around the dragon's recess.

I am nearly on top of Mount Wisdom now. I am scarred, sore and tired. I am filthy. My garment hardly looks like a golden garment since it is coated with soot and ash, and with the dirt and the grime from this climb. I am not ready to face the Climbers on Mount Wisdom yet. It would be humiliating for me to make my entrance looking like this.

The top of the Mount is so close that I know I will reach it on my next climb. I have not seen a dragon for three days, so I assume I am above them now. I am very, very tired.

I will rest for a day or two and then see what this climb was all about – what Mount Wisdom has to offer.

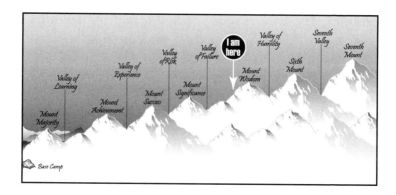

21

Now I know me better.

My arrival on Mount Wisdom was not what I expected. On Mount Success and on Mount Significance the Climbers there were continuously encouraging each other. They congratulated each other frequently. There were many animated conversations and joyous celebrations. There was a great deal of laughter.

There is little of that here. It is not that the Climbers here are serious or long-faced or anything like that. They smile easily and laugh occasionally. Mostly they seem lost in their thoughts and in meaningful conversations.

Everyone here is a Teacher. I am considered to be a Teacher.

Off in the distance, Mount Servanthood is visible from anywhere on Mount Wisdom. It seems to be a constant reminder of what is to come.

It was somewhat humiliating to arrive here. Although I had cleaned myself and my garment as well as I could, I was still dirty and I smelled of burnt flesh and burnt plants. The Climbers who greeted me took my gold garment and helped me get cleaned up. They drew a tub of hot water for me and gave me soap and lotions. One trimmed my hair, another my nails. I began to feel like myself again.

I was given my new garment.

The garment we wear here is very ornate. At first I thought it was silver and I found that to be a bit odd. It turns out that the base metal for the garments is platinum. On the chest of the garment there are precious stones, twelve in all. They are large and are held in place with bronze clasps. Each person's garment has a different mix and arrangement of stones.

Mine has diamonds, rubies emeralds and sapphires.

There is gold trim in various places. Again, every person has a different garment. I have massive gold embroidery on my cuffs and on my shoulders.

I have a belt woven of pure silver strands. Each strand is a braid made of many smaller strands.

This is by far the most comfortable and the most regal garment I have had.

As on the other Mounts, there is one Teacher here that seems to be the most knowledgeable. She is known as "The Wise One". I sought her out and asked for some time with her. She was always busy, but I persisted. Finally she agreed to meet with me.

Her first questions were all about my climb. She asked," What did you learn?" many times. Whenever I would tell about an experience, she would inevitably follow it with, "What did you learn?"

As I talked, she smiled often and even laughed at some of the dumber things I had done – like thinking I had to sneak off of Mount Achievement. She was an encouraging listener.

We spent a full day together and I had only gotten to the

*part about climbing Mount Significance. She suggested that
we continue our conversation the following day. She also
said she was pleased with what she thought I had learned.*

*The next day The Wise One and I continued our conversa-
tion and it took a different turn.*

*I told her about my return to Mount Success from Mount
Significance and she said that was a noble thing for me to
have done.*

*As I told her about my climb through the Valley of Failure
and my encounter with the lava pits, her countenance
changed. I sensed the change but, being near the end of my
recounting, I continued.*

*When I had completed my travelogue, she asked me several
more questions about my time in the Valley of Failure. I
knew she was seeking something from me and I was not
saying what she wanted to hear.*

*Finally I stopped talking and I asked her what she was
thinking. She said she was thinking that I would have to go
back through the Valley of Failure again. I had missed
something important. She also said I would have to stay in
the Valley until I figured out what I had missed.*

*The alternative was to go back to Mount Significance and
stay there.*

*Once again, the allure of Mount Significance entered my
thoughts. On Mount Significance, everyone is significant.
While I was there, we all recognized and appreciated the
significance of the other Climbers. There was great camaraderie. We applauded and even boasted about the Signifi-*

cance of others. There was a lot to be said for staying there.

Then again, there was something inside of me that kept pushing me to continue my climb. The thought of having to pass through the Valley of Failure for any length of time was enough to cause me to reconsider my idea of returning to Significance.

Perhaps I had been right a long time ago when I thought I would stay on Mount Significance forever. Maybe I should have never left.

The Wise One sensed my thoughts. She encouraged me by reminding me that once we had conquered a valley, going back through it was never as difficult as it had been. Still, thinking back on that awful place, her words were of little consolation.

I had to decide if I wanted to stop on Mount Wisdom or continue my climb by going back and learning the lessons in the Valley of Failure.

"Stop or continue," she said, "you decide."

I climbed back down into the Valley of Failure. The new garment and the lessons I had learned when I was there before served me well. The experience was not anything like my first time in the Valley.

I had determined to go all the way back to Mount Significance, if necessary, in search of what I had missed. At least on Mount Significance I would be even more Significant wearing the garments of the Fifth Mount. Everyone there would be impressed with the garment, the stones, the trim and the belt.

Everything in the Valley of Failure seemed to be the same. The ground was parched and black. What few trees were still standing were dark and ominous. The hindrances appeared to be as sinister as ever but they did not frighten or threaten me.

I went through the Valley for weeks and was nearing Mount Significance when I had a revelation. For some reason I had looked down at my feet. They were covered in soot and ash. But my garment was as clean as when I had first put it on. I thought that might have something to do with the lesson I was seeking, but it wasn't. It only led me to the lesson.

There, beside my foot, was a small green spring. It was pushing itself up from the cinders of a burned log. I looked closer and saw that there were hundreds, maybe thousands of these sprigs. Then, as I scanned around the floor of the Valley, I saw that these springs were everywhere.

How had I missed them before?

I turned and began making my way back towards Mount Wisdom. As I walked I thought about the sprigs and how I had missed them. On my first trip through this Valley I had been concentrating on looking for the hindrances. I knew that any of the hindrances could end my quest right here in the Valley of Failure. I had not known then what the new hindrances were and so I paid close attention to anything that looked threatening.

In my efforts to protect myself from danger, I had missed the new life that was going on all around me. There was enough failure and even desolation here to discourage anyone. But there was also the hope of new life for anyone who cared to look closely enough.

I returned to Mount Wisdom and The Wise One confirmed that this was the lesson I had missed. When I arrived back on the Mount I immediately sought her out and received her confirmation. I felt great.

Then she asked for some of my time.

Of course I immediately stopped and we talked.

She told me that I was a Scout. There were not many Scouts, she said, but we were the ones who were to go ahead of others and them help them on their climb. We were to encourage them in any way we could.

I asked her if I was supposed to go all the way back to Mount Achievement and teach and encourage others. I asked if I should consider going to Mount Majority or even back to Base Camp as I had seen the Sherpas doing.

"You or your message," she said, "you decide."

"I don't understand," I said.

"Exactly," she responded. Then she smiled.

The look on my face must have told her how confused I was.

After a while she gently explained it all to me. On Mount Majority we did not know and we did not know that we did not know. On Mount Achievement, we knew that we did not know. On Mount Success we knew that we knew. On Mount Significance we understood. On Mount Wisdom we knew that we really did not understand after all.

We weren't supposed to understand, she said. One of the greatest truths we can learn is that we never truly understand much of anything. The more we know, the less we realize that we know.

True wisdom comes from a continuous quest for understanding. We do not quest for something that we already have.

Tonight as I rest in a hut, I am thinking about the conversation with The Wise One. Somehow, whatever I had learned on my climb is to be used to help other Climbers on their quest.

But what are they questing for? How am I supposed to help? Why me?

A moment ago I reflected back on one of my first conversations with myself. It was when I was climbing Mount Majority and I wondered if this is all the luck of the draw or the grace of God.

It is neither.

This was my quest. Everyone has their own quest. This is mine. And yet, everyone must pass through the seven Valleys and climb the seven Mounts to complete their quests.

No one's calling is complete if they have not climbed the Seventh Mount.

It then occurred to me that I had not seen any other Climber keeping a journal. Perhaps this journal is the message.

I know now that my quest will not end until I have climbed the Seventh Mount. Between here and there are Mount Servanthood and the valleys in-between the Mounts. Whatever they are, I will conquer them.

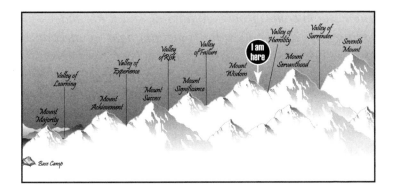

22

I am gratefully humiliated.

I asked The Wise One a final question before continuing my climb to Mount Servanthood. I wanted to ask what the aggressive and the passive hindrances would be in the next Valley, the Valley of Humility. Instinctively I knew that she would not answer that question.

So, instead, I asked her what advice she would give me for my climb.

"You will meet your greatest foe," she said.

I began my climb.

The new garment gave me a renewed sense of confidence. The lessons learned on Mount Wisdom gave me great resolve. Knowing my quest gave me a great sense of purpose.

All of the hindrances of the previous valleys were also there in the Valley of Humility. According to The Wise One, there would be a new aggressive hindrance, my greatest foe, and there would be a new passive hindrance.

I had learned to ward off the insects. I walked casually through the brambles, almost like a Sherpa. I was very good at sensing when a snake or tiger was nearby and I knew how to handle them. Swamps and quicksand were no longer threats to me. Whenever I sensed that the temperature was rising, I immediately began looking for lava pits and dragons. My senses, my intuition, had been honed during my climb and I was learning to trust them.

The foliage in the Valley of Humility was lush and huge. Giant trees formed a canopy high above me. Beautiful plants were everywhere. The fruit there was indescribable. It reminded me of what the Garden of Eden must have looked like.

In only a few days it seemed I had reached the base of Mount Servanthood and I had not encountered any new hindrances. Was the climb finally becoming easier?

Because of the trees I could not see very far up the mountain but I began my climb anyway. I was still watching out for the new hindrances, of course. I felt a sense of elation that this Valley had been so easy to cross.

That is when the ground began to shake. I heard a loud roar like the growl of a giant. This was followed by a loud explosion and then flaming rocks began raining down where I was standing.

Stunned, I stood still for a moment trying to figure out what was happening. It took a huge chunk of flaming rock to start me running. I was at the foot of a volcano, not at the base of Mount Servanthood.

I began running. First I would run in one direction. When a shower of flaming rocks would rain down I would run in another direction to get away for them. I changed courses so many times that I could no longer tell if I was running towards Mount Servanthood or away from it. I was completely disoriented.

All I knew to do was run.

Then I heard a roar behind me. It was not as loud as the

one I had heard earlier but it was constant – and ominous. As I continued to run I looked back over my shoulder and saw a wall of molten lava flowing right towards me.

I did not know if I could outrun it.

I thought about climbing a tall tree and trying to get above the lava but then remembered that the tree would burn instantly.

My garment was now a problem. In addition to its weight, it was becoming hotter by the moment.

First I decided to risk snakebites by removing the belt and leggings.

That was not enough so I decided to risk the tiger and dragon attacks and tore off the sleeves as I continued to run.

It still was not enough.

I was not about to remove the breastplate with the beautiful stones and gold accents. This was far too precious. It was my badge of honor. It was the possession of only a select few. It must be saved at all costs.

I had earned the breastplate. All of the time spent in the different Valleys and all of the pain I had suffered in conquering the hindrances had given me the right to have this. It would not be taken from me.

Besides, my knapsack was tied to the back of the breastplate and I did not want to risk losing that.

As hard as I could run, the lava was gaining on me. I tried zigzagging but the lava had only gotten closer. Hadn't I learned anything on the climb up Mount Majority when I watched other Climbers waste time by zigzagging?

Soon I could actually hear the sizzling and the popping deep inside the lava flow. I was about to give up when I saw a large lake ahead. The water in the lake – if it was water – would cool the lava. I was a pretty good swimmer so I should be able to swim far enough and fast enough to escape.

Thinking back, it must have been quite a sight. Here is a Climber, naked from the waist down, barely in front of a huge lava flow running as fast as possible for a lake. If anyone had seen that it would have been the height of humiliation for me, or so I thought.

The skin on the back of my legs was seared as I jumped into the water. But rather than swimming to safety, I sank like a rock. The breastplate was dragging me down. Without hesitation I slipped out of it and swam with all my strength.

I never saw the breastplate again.

The lava flow hit the water with such force that the wave it created actually propelled me and some of the floating debris out into the lake.

When I was sure I was far enough away, I turned around in the water and looked back at the volcano. It had stopped its eruption and was becoming quiet again. Steam rose up in the water where the lava flow had already begun cooling.

I swam to shore, lay down on the bank of the lake and

considered my plight.

I now lacked even the most basic garments and any tools. I had no more possessions now than I had on the day I was born.

As I lay on my back letting the sun dry me, I became aware of a shadow across my face. I opened my eyes and saw a Sherpa. He was staring into my eyes, as they always do, but I still tried to hide myself from him. I had never been naked in front of a Sherpa before.

"Start over or quit," he said, "you decide."

With that he was gone.

I thought about his message and then I got up and started over. I fashioned some green garments, the type that the Climbers on Mount Majority wear. I was starting over, it seemed, from where I had been on Mount Majority. But I was still further along than I had been when I was in Base Camp.

I climbed the tallest tree I could find and got my bearings. I saw Mount Servanthood off in the distance and began walking in that direction.

Eating a lot of fruit warded off the insects and it made me feel better. I watched for snakes and tigers and made a point to stay in the low grass where they could not hide. I avoided swamps, lava pits and quicksand easily enough, but it meant taking extremely long routes instead of short-cuts.

Eventually it happened: I faced a tiger. As usual, it happened suddenly. The beast lunged at me and, out of reflex, I raised my arm as if to hit it with the sleeve of my garment. But there was no sleeve. Despite that, the tiger did a back flip, landed on the ground and I completed the task of taking him out.

A couple of other tigers appeared over the next few days and were dealt with the same way. I learned that it wasn't the garments that made me safe.

I was surprised at how quickly the base of Mount Servanthood appeared. I guess I had been concentrating on the difficulty of the climb and trying to protect myself and had lost track of time. Still, the Mount came within my reach not soon, but suddenly.

I had not faced a dragon and I knew that if there were any in this Valley, they would be in the recesses on the Mount. What was I to do?

It was clear to me that I was not going back through the Valley of Humiliation. I had lost my journal so my quest was apparently over. This might be the end.

Once again I was facing the death of myself and this time there was no real reason for me to win. My role as a Scout seemed to have ended.

I called for a Sherpa. For several hours I called out but instinctively I knew that no Sherpa would come to help. This was a challenge I would need to face alone.

This was my moment of truth. I had to face the dragons. I had to face them alone. If I survived, I had earned a place on Mount Servanthood, and maybe beyond. If not, I had given my climb – my quest – my best effort.

The ascent of Mount Servanthood was a pleasant surprise. Rather than jagged rocks and sheer stone faces, the Mount was mostly rounded mounds. What was also strange was that the ground was not hard but soft – it actually gave gently as I walked. It occurred to me that I could climb for hours without rest on such terrain. So I did.

Was this the reward for my diligence? Was the climb to the ultimate realization of truth and wisdom now becoming easier? It would seem to make sense. For anyone to reach this point they would have had to fight and suffer many difficulties. Perhaps it was too much to expect anyone to be able to negotiate more difficult perils at this stage of their climb.

I looked down and saw the scars on the back of my hand. There were scars from the burns of previous dragons and scars from tiger claws. There were scars from the briars. The back of my hand was a living testimonial to what I had experienced on my climb. It was not as if my entire life flashed before my eyes, it was more like my quest and my purpose became clearly focused in that moment.

Finally, I stopped to rest and sat on the edge of a small, smooth, rounded bank. It gave way slightly as I sat, the same way a good chair gives way.

Then it happened. In an instant the face of an enormous creature rose up and stared directly at me. It had the face of a terrible cat, teeth with fangs like a poisonous serpent, and eyes that pierced my eyes with the satisfaction that I was its prey. It could spit fire like a dragon or venom like a snake. At will, it could maim me, mutilate me or bring a swift or a slow death. It could render me helpless, useless, hideous in appearance. With one flick of its tongue it could wipe out my ability to see, hear, speak – or even think. It embodied every fear I had ever faced. In one foul creature there was everything a man could dread.

I had not been sitting on the ground nor had I been climbing on the mount. This creature has completely covered the Mount with its enormous body which was now uncoiling. Part dragon, part serpent, this embodiment of evil was about to end my climb and I was so close to the final Mount.

Instinctively I reached for my weapons and attempted to straighten my breastplate. All were gone, of course. The surface below me began to give way as the creature moved. Yelling for a Sherpa was not an option – somehow I knew that. This creature would have to be defeated by what was inside of me.

A new resolve boiled up in me. Nothing was going to stop me.

I stood, faced the creature and began walking towards him, never taking my eyes off of his. It began slowly moving backwards. While his tongue flicked around his snout and venom dripped from its fangs, it never once tried to strike at me.

This continued for what seemed to be a lifetime. I would move towards its head, it would move backwards. Subconsciously, I think, I had begun taking steps that would move me higher on the Mount. Without realizing it, I had begun walking on real rocks.

Fatigue began to set in and I was not sure how much longer I could continue this intense encounter. So I took a step towards the creature, waved my arm as widely as I could and shouted "Be gone!".

The stillness of the Mount amazed me. In an instant the creature and all of its accompanying distractions was gone. Sounds I had not been aware of that were a part of the creature had disappeared along with the roaring and hissing. Now all I could hear was the wind in the trees, the sound of a waterfall off in the distance and the occasional call of one bird to another.

From somewhere a Voice, the only way I know to describe it is "a Voice", spoke and said, "Speak the Word and the Work of your Hands is established".

The power to overcome the creatures is courage, not garments.

Courage is having faith and being obedient to that faith.

Obedience includes speaking the Word.

Speaking the Word includes knowing the Word in order to know what to speak.

So what does this mean, this encounter, this victory on Mount Servanthood? What I have concluded so far – and I expect to learn more on the climb – is this: serving is giving of self. It is not having the right weapons or the best garments, it is using what has been instilled inside of us. I do not know where the idea of waving my arm and yelling,

"Be gone" come from, other than to say that it came from within me.

The trials, failures and successes of the climb so far have instilled in me what I need to be a servant. Future lessons will teach me to be a better servant. Serving on one occasion may involve fighting and I am prepared for that. Other times, serving may involve teaching or mentoring. Mostly, though, serving will be about helping others on their climb.

Maybe I become a Sherpa?

After three or four days of climbing – and meditating, I assumed that I was near the top of Mount Servanthood. I was right.

I was very tired. My green garments had long since turned brown. I was dirty. Actually, I was as filthy as I had ever been.

Two Climbers appeared. They were wearing simple white garments. They walked with a lilt in their step. They chatted with each other as they made their way to where I was taking a break.

A fleeting thought went through my mind that I should hide or cover myself or something. After all, back on Mount Majority a brown garment brings humiliation to the wearer. But now, it just does not matter anymore.

They continued to talk with each other as one of them handed me a garment like the ones they were wearing. One of the Climbers pointed to a stream just off to one side of where we were. They turned and began walking back up the slope to the top of the Mount, still chatting.

I went over to the stream, bathed and put on the white garment. Then I climbed to see what awaited me on Mount Servanthood.

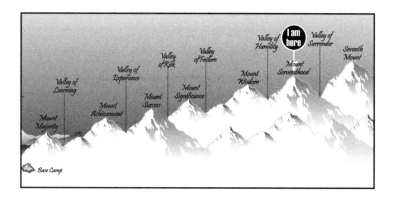

23

Lessons from the Sage.

I have been on Mount Servanthood for seven months. Three months ago, a Sherpa came up from the Valley of Humility carrying my knapsack. He said he had found it on the lakeshore. The rush of the lava flow must have pushed it out of harm's way with the other floating debris.

I have taken the time to dry the pages and make the previous entry from memory.

I am anxious to complete my climb through the Seventh Valley and up to the top of the Seventh Mount. I take my assignment as a Scout seriously and so I want to make sure that I have the message written out as clearly as possible.

What I have learned since arriving on Mount Servanthood has made the climb more than worthwhile.

As on the other Mounts, there is a Master Teacher here who is affectionately called the Sage. He is a Climber like the rest of us. He is gifted with incredible wisdom – some call it supernatural – and with infinite patience.

He is a most remarkable teacher. Sometimes he teaches the lesson and other times he causes the listener to learn the lesson. He always seems to know which method is the best in any given situation.

There is no way to record all of his teachings because they continue flow all day and everyday.

Everyone here dresses the same way and after a while, no one notices. What we wear is of little importance. There are no bronze, silver, gold or platinum garments here. And there are no precious stones.

On lower Mounts, a Climber's worth is often measured by what is on the outside. That is why the garments on higher Mounts are different and seemingly better. Once a Climber has come face-to-face with true humility, their need for outer manifestations of achievement goes away.

No one here seems to be in a rush to do anything for themselves. Yet they are anxious to do things for others. They seek out ways to help each other. The Climbers here are more helpful than any of the Climbers I have encountered anywhere else.

Their help is usually more practical than just an encouraging word.

In one-on-one conversations with the Sage and from discussions involving the Sage and others, here are some of the more important lessons for me.

We all begin at Base Camp.

We are all born with an innate desire to reach the Seventh Mount. Many allow hindrances to stop them. Some allow other Climbers to talk them out of their quest. Those who attempt the climb to the Seventh Mount do so at their own risk. Some fail, some are wounded, some die.

Those who do not attempt this sacred climb are dead already.

*There are no rich or smart Climbers, there is no royalty
and there is no distinction in Climbers at all after Mount
Majority. That is the Mount where lesser thoughts and
smaller ambitions are tolerated and even encouraged. Only
a few move beyond it. Few learn that position, power and
material wealth are, in fact, worthless on the Seventh
Mount.*

*In each Valley we encounter an element of our quest. When
we have made it through that Valley, we think we have mastered that element. It is actually the next valley where that
element will be taught.*

*In the second valley, the Valley of Learning, it seemed we
mastered tough experiences. We did not. It was the next
Valley, the Valley of Experience where that lesson really
happened.*

*In the third Valley, the Valley Experience, we had to take
great risks. However, it was not until we reached the Fourth
Valley, the Valley of Risk that we truly had to overcome
risks.*

*In the Valley of Risk, everyone fails yet we do not truly face
our failures until we reach the next Valley, the Valley of
Failure.*

*Anyone who has been in the Valley of Failure has suffered
some of the most humiliating situations of their life. Yet it is
the Valley of Humility where we learn true humility.*
*In the Valley of Humility, we think we have lost it all. No
one has emerged from this Valley with anything. Yet it is the
Seventh Valley, the Valley of Sacrifice where we truly lay it
all down.*

Most of the physical attacks come to our feet. Every Climber on Mount Servanthood has feet that are bruised and scarred from burns, scratches and cuts. The reason for this is that our feet represent our foundation. We stand on our feet. Our feet hold us erect. And when we go anywhere or do almost anything, our feet take us there. Our foundation is what needs to be strengthened and tested. And it needs to be purified by fire.

One day when the Sage and I were alone, I asked him about the Sixth Valley, the Valley of Humiliation. I had been challenged by the volcano, the aggressive hindrance, but could not remember facing a new passive hindrance in that Valley.

The Sage sat beside me and smiled, as he often did. He thought for a moment so I knew this would be a time of learning for me. Finally he said, "The volcano was the passive hindrance."

I thought about how the volcano had spewed rocks at me and how the lava flow had chased me. That did not seem like a passive hindrance. Besides, The Wise One had said I would face the toughest hindrance yet and the volcano seemed to be that.

Still, the Sage was the wisest among all of the Climbers here, so I took his word. Then I asked, "Well, then what was the aggressive hindrance – the toughest foe I would ever face?"

The Sage looked me in the eye and said nothing.

It was me. I was my own greatest hindrance.

In every Valley and on every Mount, I was the one who was

getting in my way. I was the one who thought of giving up and quitting and I did that several times. I was the one who thought I needed the garments, especially the one with the precious stones in order to be who I was destined to be.

The garments were not necessary for survival among any of the hindrances. After all, other Climbers who had similar garments perished all along the climb. The Climber who went after the too-good-to-be-true fruit, perished in the quicksand. It was get-rich-quicksand.

There was the Climber who tried to pet the tiger. His own foolishness in letting his guard down cost him his life.

I do not know how many Climbers in their gold garments perished in the lava pit. But there had to be many for the gold ring to be there as a reminder. Their own cleverness brought them down as mine almost had.

The last two Valleys, the Valley of Failure and the Valley of Humility both had hindrances of fire: lava pits, dragons and volcanoes. The reason for this, according to the Sage, is that in precious metals, fire burns out the dross, or impurities. Once a Climber has reached the Valley of Failure, they are considered to be special, extremely valuable – or <u>precious</u>. They must then be purified and it is the trial by fire that brings the purification.

The Sage said this is the last Mount before the Seventh Mount. The next Valley, the Valley of Sacrifice, is where the Climber will be asked to lay down everything that is worldly. Once a Climber does that, they can ascend the Seventh Mount. None will ever want to return. He did not say none has ever returned; only that none would want to.

Every Climber here wants to serve. They do things for each other. They make frequent trips back through the other Valleys to the lower Mounts and perform their good deeds.

It seemed strange that I could never recall seeing one of these Climbers in white garments when I was on a lower Mount or in any of the valleys.

The Sage explained this as well. He said that the value in serving was to serve without being known or noticed. If anyone saw them doing their good deed, the deed did not count. It was only when the deed was done secretly or when a gift was given anonymously that it was real Servanthood.

I asked why these Climbers did not continue on to the Seventh Mount. The Sage said that they would all go there eventually. But most had found this to be the best time of their lives. They were enjoying living now more than they ever had before. They each wanted to experience more of the joy of serving before moving on.

After this conversation, I made a few trips down as far as Mount Success and secretly did some things for the Climbers there who had done good things for me and good things for others. They probably never knew why those big and little "gifts" came their way. But one day, when they have reached Mount Servanthood, they will know.

I think I am ready for the final part of my climb.

24

Final entry – unless I return from the Seventh Mount.

Later this morning I will begin making my way to the Seventh Mount. As a responsible Scout, if there is anything to report and if I can report it to you, I will.

This morning the Sage came by to wish me well. We were sitting at the edge of Mount Servanthood, looking out at the Seventh Mount and speaking to the Climbers who were beginning their climb through the Valley of Sacrifice. The Sage greeted each one.

"God be with you."

"Shalom."

"Godspeed."

Sometimes he made the sign of the cross on his chest.

Seeing the Seventh Mount out in the distance, I wondered how anyone could resist continuing his or her climb there. It was far and away the most beautiful and majestic Mount of all.

The slopes up the side of the Mount seemed gentle. They were covered with all types of massive fruit trees.

The Seventh Mount was so high that the peak was always in a cloud – a brilliant opal-like cloud. The Mount itself stood like a giant uncut gem, one whose colors changed with the rising and setting of the sun. And the colors – they were more brilliant and translucent than anything I had experienced.

I looked back towards the Climbers on Mount Servanthood as they began their day.

For the first time I noticed something. One of the Climbers was a slight man with short gray hair and dark skin. He looked like Gandhi. Another looked like the pictures I had seen of Mohammed. One looked like Mother Theresa. As I looked at the others, many of them also looked like Biblical characters and other great people – great givers – from history.

I looked at the Sage. "So no one has ever returned from the Seventh Mount?"

The Sage smiled and thought for a moment. This would be a learning experience. "One did. He did many great things and many, many people now follow in his footsteps."

He thought for a moment and then added, "And many more will."

"So who was he?"

You decide.